RUTHIE AND JOE GIVE
THEIR LIVES TO JESUS

Story by Coretha Gantling

Illustrations by Coretha, Ruthie, and Joe

Published by:

Little Oaks Publishing
www.thepublishedword.com

ISBN: 978-1-964665-14-6

Printed on demand in the U.S., the U.K. and Australia
For Worldwide Distribution

This book is dedicated to Ruth, Joseph, and their grandfather, Franklin Harvey, in honor of Mima (Angela Harvey), their grandmother and his wife, who went home to be with the Lord in August of 2024. She will always be remembered with love.

Ruthie and Joe with their grandfather

Chapter 1

OUR WONDERFUL PARENTS

Hello, my name is Joseph, Joe for short. My sister's name is Ruth, and we call her Ruthie. Our parents, Franklin and Angelia Harvey, love us very much and have taught us about God, Jesus, and the Holy Spirit since we can remember. Our mom sings like an angel, and our dad plays the keyboard and the base guitar with a calming rhythm.

On Sunday mornings, our parents take us to the children's ministry at our church, where they are the lead teachers. They keep us laughing and on the edge of our seats as they teach us in fun, creative ways that bring stories from Bible days alive. As our classmates' parents bring them to the children's ministry class, they often say they hear an angel singing and the songs sound so heavenly, They hear our mom teaching us Bible songs and our dad playing the songs on the keyboard.

These are songs such as "Jesus Loves Me," "This Little Light of Mine," "I'm in the Lord's Army," and others. It's not unusual to see our dad and mom dressed in clothes that tell the story of Bible characters like David and Goliath, Ruth and Naomi, Daniel and His Friends, Joseph, Mary and the Baby Jesus, Joseph the Dreamer, and many other Bible characters.

You simply must make a special trip to visit our children's ministry and see the amazing room décor we have. Each month, depending on the story that is being told and illustrated that month, the room is decorated to help our Bible stories come alive. Every month we have amazing decorative room settings from the Bible.

You can probably guess that in the month of December we have a manger that has baby Jesus in it with Joseph and Mary next to it. There are also three wise men, stars lit up, and all that goes with that wonderful story.

Chapter 2

A CELEBRATION OF HONOR

Hi, I'm Ruthie, Joes's sister, to tell you how we celebrated our mom and dad. At the end of each month, they ask the other parents to bring their children on a Saturday to help decorate the room so that it's prepared for the next Bible story. They make that Saturday a fun day with healthy snacks and lots of water to drink. Mom is an excellent seamstress, so she also makes clothes for the children to wear to represent the Bible character for each month. One year she made outfits for the story of Daniel and his friends, and she made lion outfits for the lions to wear in the lion's den. Dad creates the sound effects for

Papas' guitar

ELECTRIC GUITARS

Artist Ruth/Ruthie

Papas' guitar

Artist Joseph/Joe

each Bible story, using the keyboard and his electric guitar.

It seems like yesterday that we were preparing for the next month's Bible stories one Saturday, and the parents of the children's ministry came to give our parents a surprise appreciation party. We had so much food we all had some to take home. The parents had gotten one of the caterers from our church to prepare the food. Since the children in our children's ministry are from different countries, we had food from Thailand, India, Jamaica, Nigeria, Belgium, Sierra Leone, Cuba, and several other countries. Our taste buds were tingling with the most delicious dishes from each country. Each of us did a presentation for our teachers and our parents. For their part, our parents taught us something we could say to honor them.

There are twenty children in our children's ministry class, and each of our classmates did an excellent presentation to show how much they appreciated their parents. Then the whole class made a beautiful mural with THE FRUIT OF THE SPIRIT on it. The mural was made up of felt squares and it had one of the fruits of the spirit on each square.

THE FRUIT OF THE SPIRIT

1. LOVE / BANANAS

2. JOY / ORANGES

3. PEACE / PEACH

4. PATIENCE / PINEAPPLE

5. KINDNESS / KIWI

6. GOODNESS / GRAPES

7. FAITHFULNESS / APPLE

8. GENTLENESS / PEAR

9. SELF-CONTROL / STRAWBERRIES

Chapter 3

OUR SALVATION STORY

This is Joe again. Weekly in our children's ministry, our parents talk to us about the importance of giving our lives to Jesus and living for Him. The first scripture we leaned by heart was John 3:16, which says:

For God so loved the world that He gave His one and only Son, that whoever believes in Him shall not perish but have everlasting life.

Mom and Dad took turns explaining that scripture to us. They explained it in sections. They explained that our dads and moms love us, but that God loves us even more that our parents love us. I said to Ruthie, "That's a lot of love," and she agreed with me. God gave us all life and His amazing love, and He wants us to love Him with all our heart, soul, and strength.

1. **God loves us.** John 3:16 shows us that by sacrificing His Son, Jesus, for us, God showed us how much He loves us.

2. **God accepts us by His mercy.**

3. **God gives us eternal life in Heaven when we believe in Jesus.** I said to Ruthie, "I believe in Jesus, don't you?" Ruthie answered, "Of course I do, Joe, and our parents do too."

4. **God offers us salvation.** God wants us to ask forgiveness for our sins (things we did that are wrong) and give our lives to Jesus and live for Him. Romans 3:23-24 states:

For all have sinned and fall short of the glory of God, and all are justified freely by His grace through the redemption that came by Christ Jesus.

I asked God to forgive me for always arguing with Ruthie when we disagree on something.

NEXT, WE LEARNED FIVE TIPS THAT CAN HELP LEAD CHILDREN TO CHRIST:

1. **Reading the Bible together with them.** Families can read the Bible together at home. Our dad and mom read and study the Bible with us every day for at least thirty minutes.

2. **Praying together.** Pray together every day. Dad and Mom pray, and they taught us to pray too. Because of that, Ruthie and I love to pray. We pray for our parents and for our whole family—

our grandparents, our uncles, our aunts, and our cousins. We also pray for the children in our church in the children's ministry.

3. **Teaching the Gospel and explaining it so your children can understand.** I love to study the Bible and learn about different Bible characters. For instance, I enjoy hearing the story about Joseph and His Coat of Many Colors. Ruthie's favorite story is from the book of Ruth. She likes the fact that Ruth loved her mother-in-law and said to her, "Your God will be my God, and wherever you go I will go too."

4. **Being an example.** Parents should live faithful lives as examples to their children. Our parents teach us by their everyday lives at home, in our neighborhood, and everywhere we go.

5. **Connecting with your church.** This way, they can get the Word of God at home and at church.

As I said, we learn so much about the Bible in our children's ministry at church.

One day Ruthie and I were reading our Bibles, and we came across the scripture that says:

As they went on their way, they came into a certain water; and the eunuch said, "Here is water, what is hindering me from being baptized?" Acts 8:36

I said to Ruthie, "Do you want to be saved today?"

She answered, "Yes, Joe. I'm so glad you asked me that because I've been thinking I wanted to give my life to Jesus. Joe, let's get baptized together."

"Okay, Ruthie," I said, "that's a very good idea."

After Ruthie and I decided to get saved, we told our parents, and they were so excited Mom started crying tears of joy. I think only adults understand what that means. So we wouldn't worry, Dad said to us, "She is so happy she is crying tears of joy."

Our parents called our bishop and told him that Ruthie and I wanted to give our lives to Jesus, and he told them to bring us to the church in a couple of hours. Joe and I were so excited we couldn't wait to get there. When we went inside, Bishop and his wife were in the sanctuary where the baptismal pool was. They wanted to talk to us before we changed clothes to get ready to be baptized.

Bishop took my hand first and said, "Joe, the Bible says if you confess with your mouth that Jesus is Lord and believe in your heart that God raised Jesus from the dead, you shall be saved. For with the heart man believeth unto righteousness, and with the mouth confession is made unto salvation." That was from Romans 10:9-10:

IF THOU SHALL CONFESS WITH THY
MOUTH THE LORD JESUS AND SHALL
BELIEVE IN THINE HEART THAT GOD
HAS RAISED HIM FROM THE DEAD,
THOU SHALT BE SAVED. FOR WITH
THE HEART MAN BELIEVETH UNTO
RIGHTEOUSNESS, AND WITH THE
MOUTH CONFESSION IS MADE UNTO
SALVATION.

Then Bishop asked me first, "do you believe in your heart that God raised Jesus from the dead?"

I said, "Yes, I do."

Next, he asked Ruthie the same question and she said yes too. Dad then took me to the men's bathroom and helped me put on some baptismal clothes, and Mom took Ruthie into the ladies' bathroom and helped her get dressed too. To me, it seemed like it took us hours to get ready, but it was only a few minutes.

Finally, it was time to get into the baptismal pool, and Ruthie was told to get in first. She was a little afraid, but Bishop's wife kept reassuring her that everything was all right. Everyone sang "Just As I Am," and then Ruthie got into the pool. Bishop took her hand and said, "Ruth, Do you believe Jesus Christ is the Son of God and your Savior?"

"Yes," she said.

Then he said, "I baptize you in the name of the Father, and of the Son, and of the Holy Spirit," and he put her under the water.

They all began to sing, "I Surrender All" as Bishop pulled Ruthie up out of the water and led her out of the pool. Mom was right there at the edge of the pool waiting to take her to the bathroom to dry off and change into dry clothes. But before they went for the dry clothes, she toweled Ruthie off and they stood to the side waiting for Bishop to do the same process with me. It was now my turn to experience what Ruthie had just experienced. I got in the pool and went through, step-by-step, what she had just done. When I came up, Dad was right there to take me to the bathroom to dry off and put on fresh clothes.

Chapter 4

OUR NEW LIFE IN CHRIST: AN AFTER-SALVATION CELEBRATION

Much to our surprise, our parents had planned an after-salvation party for us. It was held at a hotel after children's church that next Sunday. Lots of other children from our children's ministry and their families came, as well as our grandparents, uncles, aunts, and cousins. Ruthie and I had learned to swim when we were babies. Our parents took us to swimming classes for babies. So we both love the water and we both swim like fish.

Our parents had our salvation party catered. We had homemade strawberry ice cream, vanilla ice cream, and chocolate ice cream. We had all kinds of fruits: watermelon, strawberries, cantaloupe, grapes, and blue berries. We had homemade pizza. Homemade lemonade, and lots of water. We had the most delicious have-it-your-way pizza. We were allowed to put our own toppings on it. I put fruit on one piece and on the other I put chicken, Italian sausage, red bell pepper, and a few other toppings.

Our parents had a large cake made with a photo of Ruthie and me on it. The cake was so large they said it would serve a hundred people. We also had a hundred cupcakes. Fifty of the cupcakes had "Congratulations, Joe," written on them with icing, and the other fifty had "Congratulations, Ruth." They also served angel eggs and all kinds of chips and we all had so much fun!

Then, a most phenomenal thing happened! One of our classmates from our children's church said to Ruthie, "I want to get baptized too." Ruthie told me, and we told our parents. They talked to the parents of the little girl. She was nine years old too, like Ruthie. Her parents said,

"Of course she can get baptized." When everyone heard this good news, four more children wanted to be baptized. We were so glad Bishop and his wife had come so they could baptize these other children. Bishop took each child through the same process for baptismal that he had taken Ruthie and me through.

What a celebration we had that day! Everybody was so happy and excited about the salvation of those four children that no one wanted to go home. After each child was baptized, we all sang songs of praise to God, and we were there for a long time.

We sang "This Little Light of Mine," "Jesus Loves Me," "If You're Happy and You Know It," and others. This salvation party had started off as a celebration for Ruthie and me, but it turned out to also be a celebration for those other children who gave their lives to the Lord that day. We will always remember this grand occasion, for it was truly memorable.